UNLOCKING THE WORLD OF STOCK MARKET INVESTING: A COMPREHENSIVE GUIDE

UNLOCKING THE WORLD OF STOCK MARKET INVESTING
A COMPREHENSIVE GUIDE

QASI JAMES

Contents

4

6

Introduction

The universe of securities exchange effective money management is both enrapturing and complex, offering people the chance to develop their riches and secure their monetary future.

As worldwide business sectors proceed to develop and monetary scenes shift, the significance of understanding how to explore the securities exchange has never been more noteworthy. This thorough aide intends to demystify the complexities of securities exchange money management, giving you the information and devices expected to settle on informed choices and construct an effective venture portfolio.

1.1 Outline of Financial exchange Money management

Financial exchange money management includes trading portions of public corporations fully intent on producing a benefit. While the idea might appear to be clear, the elements of the financial exchange are diverse, impacted by a heap of variables like monetary circumstances, international occasions, and corporate execution. Financial backers take part in this powerful commercial center to exploit open doors and influence their monetary assets.

Understanding the securities exchange requires digging into the center ideas of stocks and the systems that drive market developments. Stocks address possession in an organization, and the securities exchange fills in as a stage where financial backers can exchange these proprietorship stakes. This guide will unwind the layers of financial exchange complexities, engaging you to grasp the basics and intricacies that underlie fruitful money management.

1.2 Significance of Putting resources into Stocks

Putting resources into stocks is a basic part of establishing financial stability and monetary preparation. Dissimilar to conventional bank accounts that proposition restricted returns, putting resources into the financial exchange gives the possibility to significant increases over the long haul. All things considered, stocks have outflanked other resource classes, offering a pathway to capital appreciation and abundance gathering.

Additionally, stock market investing provides a unique means of contributing to the expansion of global economies. As organizations flourish and grow, so do the worth of their stocks. Financial backers can adjust their monetary advantages to the progress of imaginative organizations, adding to monetary development while receiving the rewards of their speculation keenness.

1.3 Dangers and Prizes

While the likely compensations of financial exchange effective financial planning are captivating, it is fundamental to recognize and deal with the inborn dangers. The instability of monetary business sectors implies that costs can change quickly, impacted by a horde of outside factors. Because it enables you to make informed decisions, implement risk management strategies, and navigate market uncertainties, understanding risk is an essential component of becoming a successful investor.

Compensations in securities exchange effective financial planning go past money related gains. Effective financial backers frequently experience a feeling of achievement, monetary freedom, and the capacity to support life objectives like training, homeownership, and retirement. This guide will furnish you with the information to work out some kind of harmony among chance and prize, encouraging a versatile and prosperous speculation venture.

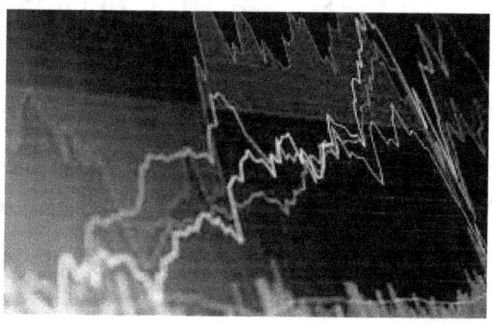

We will go over the fundamentals of stocks, the workings of the stock market, and how to set investment goals that are in line with your financial goals in the following sections. Whether you are a fledgling trying to set out on your speculation process or an accomplished financial backer hoping to refine your technique, this guide is intended to be your far reaching sidekick in the thrilling universe of securities exchange effective money management. How about we set out on this advancing excursion together, opening the capability of the securities exchange and making ready to monetary achievement.

2. Getting a handle on the monetary trade

2.1 Basics of Stocks

2.1.1 What Are Stocks?

At its middle, a stock tends to ownership in an association. Exactly when you own a part of an association's stock, you become a financial backer, giving you a case on a piece of the association's assets and benefit. There are regularly two primary kinds of stocks: pervasive and Favored investors for the most part don't cast a ballot however have a more noteworthy case on resources and profit than normal investors do. Normal investors have casting a ballot rights in organization choices.

2.1.2 Stock Images and Tickers

Every publicly traded company has a striking stock image or ticker.

These pictures are short mixes of letters that address the association on stock exchanges. For example, Apple Inc. is customarily perceived by the ticker picture AAPL. Understanding these pictures is essential while following stock expenses and going with adventure decisions.

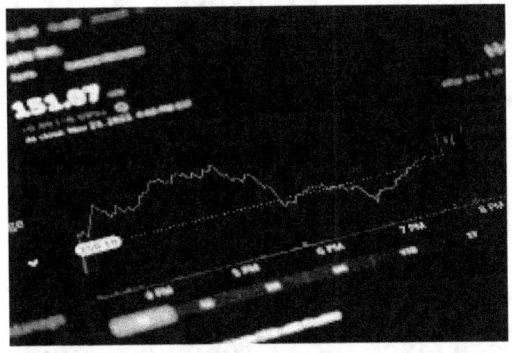

2.1.3 Market Capitalization

Market capitalization (market cap) is the full scale worth of an association's amazing segments of stock. Not set in stone by expanding the stock expense by without a doubt the quantity of outstanding offers. Market cap is frequently used to divide businesses into various sizes, such as big, medium, and small.

2.2 How the Monetary trade Capabilities

2.2.1 Stock Exchanges

Stocks are exchanged on stock exchanges, which are stages where buyers and sellers get together to trade. Critical stock exchanges integrate the New York Stock Exchange (NYSE) and the Nasdaq. Associations list their stocks on these exchanges to give monetary benefactors a brought together and oversaw business community.

2.2.2 Exchanging Stocks

Stock trades occur through delegates, who go about as go

betweens among buyers and vendors. Monetary patrons can put solicitations to exchange stocks through these dealers, and trades are executed electronically on the exchange. Market orders are executed at the continuous business area cost, while limit orders license monetary supporters to show the expense at which they will exchange.

2.2.3 Bull and Bear Markets

Market designs are often depicted as bull or bear markets. An emphatically moving business sector is separate by rising stock expenses, cheerfulness, and monetary patron sureness. Curiously, declining costs, cynicism, and a general lack of certainty characterize a bear market. Understanding these examples helps monetary benefactors with making educated decisions in view regarding the general market feeling.

2.3 Key Protections trade Individuals

2.3.1 Monetary supporters

Individuals, foundations, and resources that exchange stocks the market are monetary supporters. Their trading strategies may be affected by their distinct speculation goals, risk tolerances, and time horizons.

2.3.2 Traders

Traders work with stock trades by executing orders for monetary patrons. They can be standard full-organization go-betweens or online markdown sellers, each offering different levels of organization and cost structures.

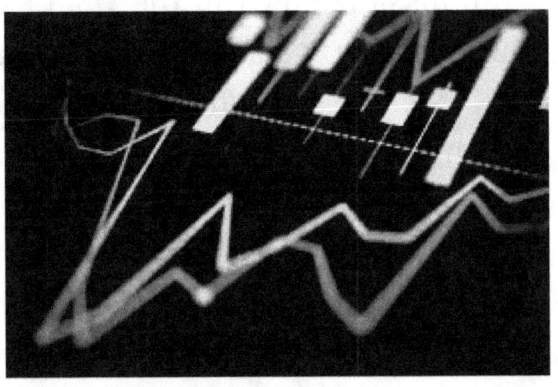

2.3.3 Market Makers

Market makers are components that work with liquidity in the market by exchanging stocks. They contribute to reducing the bid-ask spread, improving cost effectiveness, and ensuring that there is a constant progression of exchanges.

2.3.4 Regulators

Authoritative bodies, for instance, the Assurances and Exchange Commission (SEC) in the US, direct the monetary trade to ensure fair and clear trading practices. Financial backers are protected and market respectability is maintained by their guidelines.

Getting a handle on the fundamentals of stocks, the mechanics of the protections trade, and the positions of key individuals lays out the foundation for fruitful monetary trade cash the board. In the going with regions, we will research through and through assessments, for instance, key and concentrated assessment to empower you in going with informed hypothesis decisions.

3. Advancing Hypothesis Targets

3.1 Flitting versus Long stretch Targets

3.1.1 Portraying Transient Targets

Transient hypothesis targets ordinarily range one to three years and incorporate objectives that require fairly quick sponsoring. Models consolidate setting something to the side for a move away, purchasing a vehicle, or building a reinforcement stash. To guarantee that assets are promptly accessible when required, momentary ventures should put a need on dependability and liquidity.

3.1.2 Embracing Long-Term Goals

Long-term investment objectives extend beyond three years and frequently include larger monetary objectives such as financing education, purchasing a home, or building retirement savings. Long stretch successful monetary arranging thinks about a more expanded and improvement arranged approach, considering the conceivable compounding of benefits over an extensive period.

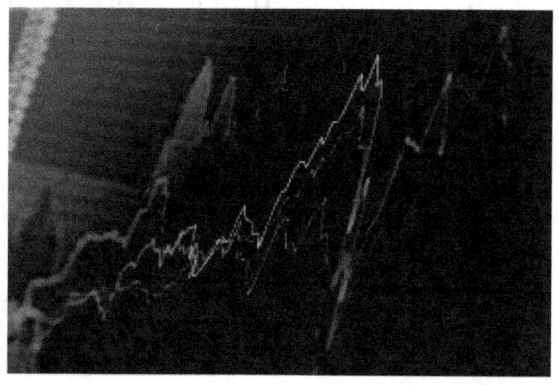

3.2 Gamble Resistance Evaluation

3.2.1 Gamble Resilience A financial backer's gamble resilience is their ability to endure changes in their speculations' worth. Reviewing your bet flexibility is a pressing push toward characterizing adventure targets, as it changes your portfolio to your comfort level and financial objectives. Factors influencing bet versatility consolidate age, money related security, and individual character.

3.2.2 Moderate versus Forceful Approaches Financial backers with a lower risk resistance may choose moderate approaches, emphasizing pay age and capital preservation. On the other hand, those alright with higher bet could seek after intense procedures, zeroing in on additional critical yields through improvement organized adventures.

3.3 Creating a Differentiated Portfolio

3.3.1 The Importance of Enhancement Spreading investments across various resource classes, ventures, and geographic regions to lessen the impact of a poor-performing investment on the overall portfolio is an aspect of enhancement. An expanded portfolio can further develop returns while directing risks related with express regions or monetary circumstances.

3.3.2 Resource Distribution Techniques Resource assignment is the most common way of sorting out the amount of your portfolio is put resources into stocks, bonds, and money. The right asset segment depends upon your hypothesis goals, risk strength, and time horizon. Ordinary techniques integrate intense, endlessly moderate parts.

3.4 Standard Review and Change

3.4.1 The Novel Thought of Goals Theory goals are dynamic and may progress after some time in light of changes in confidential circumstances, money related business areas, or monetary conditions. Reliably keeping an eye on your targets grants you to assess progress, change frameworks, and realign your portfolio with current longings.

3.4.2 Rebalancing Your Portfolio

Market changes can make your asset assignment go wrong from your arranged mix. Periodic rebalancing incorporates changing your portfolio to stay aware of the best task. This ensures that your bet profile stays as per your bet versatility and long stretch objectives.

3.5 Cost Viability

3.5.1 Sorting out Obligation Ideas

Monetary benefactors should contemplate the cost implications of their endeavor decisions. Charge misfortune collecting methods and putting resources into charge proficient assets are two methods for reducing the effect of duties on returns. Charge powerful orchestrating is particularly fundamental for enhancing after-government structures.

3.5.2 Retirement Organizing and Obligation Advantaged Records

For long stretch targets like retirement, utilizing charge advantaged accounts, for instance, 401(k)s or IRAs, can give basic tax cuts. These documents enable financial backers to advance their retirement investment funds by providing duty deferral or tax-exempt development.

All things considered, characterizing adventure targets is a fundamental push toward fostering a productive theory framework. By incorporating tax-efficient strategies, creating a diversified portfolio, evaluating risk tolerance, and clearly defining objectives, investors can construct a course toward financial success. The accompanying sections will research different monetary trade assessment techniques and adventure strategies to extra update your ability to achieve these goals.

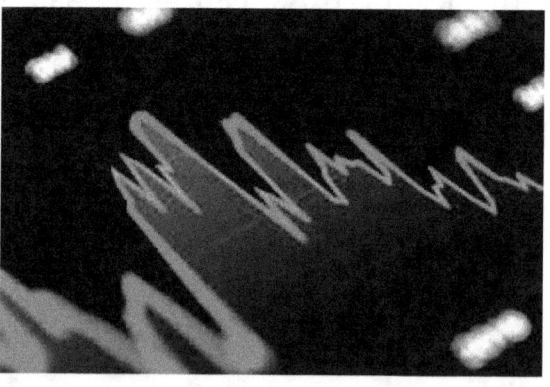

4. Protections trade Examination

4.1 Fundamental Examination

4.1.1 Pay Reports

Pay reports give encounters into an association's financial prosperity and execution. Taking apart pay, net addition, and benefit per share (EPS) helps monetary supporters with really looking at benefit. Additionally, differentiating current benefit and evident data and industry benchmarks upholds reviewing an association's for the most part financial course.

4.1.2 Financial Ratios Financial ratios like price to earnings (P/E), price to deals (P/S), and obligation to value are useful metrics for determining an organization's value and financial viability. P/E, for instance, takes a gander at the stock expense for money, helping monetary sponsor with reviewing whether a stock is overstated or underrated similar with its pay.

4.2 Particular Examination

4.2.1 Outlines and Models

Particular examination incorporates focusing on cost diagrams and recognizing guides to check future expense improvements. Typical blueprint plans consolidate head and shoulders, twofold tops and bottoms, and trend lines. These undeniable prompts help monetary sponsor with making educated decisions in light regarding unquestionable expense improvements.

4.2.2 Markers and Oscillators

Specific pointers, for instance, moving midpoints, Relative

Strength Rundown (RSI), and Moving Typical Blend Divergence (MACD), give quantitative extents of market examples and energy. These markers are used by financial backers to affirm the strength of a pattern and to recognize possible passage and leave focuses.

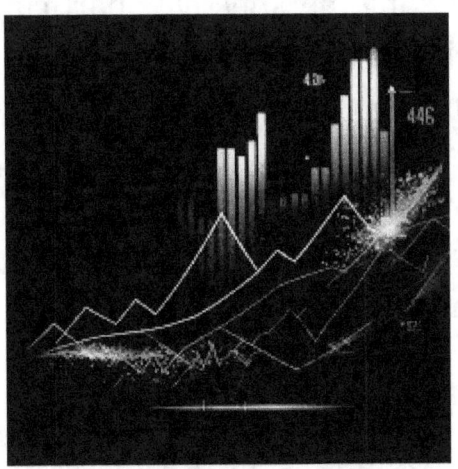

4.3 Solidifying Fundamental and Specific Assessment

4.3.1 Sweeping Route

Productive monetary supporters much of the time use a mix of key and concentrated examination to seek after adjusted decisions. While fundamental assessment gives a really long perspective, particular examination offers pieces of information into transient market improvements. A thorough understanding of a stock's true capacity is made conceivable by joining the two methodologies.

4.4 Industry Assessment

4.4.1 Looking over Business area Examples

Seeing greater industry designs is indispensable for surveying an association's improvement potential. Taking apart market components, serious scenes, and industry interferences gives setting to assessing what is happening inside its area.

4.4.2 Monetary Pointers

Really looking at money related pointers, for instance, Total national output advancement, credit expenses, and extension, helps monetary patrons with expecting macroeconomic examples that can impact express endeavors. Seeing what money related conditions mean for adventures assists with seeking after informed hypothesis decisions.

4.5 Initiative and The board

4.5.1 Assessment of the Chief Group

The assessment of a business' supervisory crew is fundamental to deciding its true capacity for progress. Experiences into the organization's ability to conquer deterrents and quickly take advantage of chances can be acquired by assessing the history of the initiative, vital choices, and corporate administration rehearses.

4.5.2 Corporate Culture and Development It is essential for long-term maintainability to examine an organization's way of life and commitment to development. Associations that develop a culture of adaptability and improvement are better arranged to thrive in propelling business area conditions.

4.6 News and Market Examples
4.6.1 Excess Informed
Keeping awake to date with late turns of events, news, and market designs is basic for making perfect

theory decisions. News can influence stock expenses, and observing basic progressions helps monetary sponsor with changing their strategies to changing financial circumstances.

4.6.2 Looking at Market Feeling News and virtual entertainment driven market opinion can affect stock costs. Separating feeling pointers and seeing multitude lead helps monetary patrons in estimating potential market advancements and changing their positions suitably.

Incorporating a fiery protections trade examination approach incorporates a comprehensive evaluation of both focal and particular variables, industry components, the leaders limits, and current market designs. We'll take a gander at an assortment of venture methodologies that work for various economic situations and financial backer inclinations in the accompanying segments.

5. Venture Systems

5.1 Worth Money management

5.1.1 Standards of Significant worth Money management

Esteem money management includes distinguishing underestimated stocks and putting resources into them with the assumption that their actual worth will be perceived after some time. Analyzing financial statements, looking for businesses with a margin of safety, and focusing on long-term holding are key principles.

5.1.2 Principal Examination in Worth Financial planning

In esteem effective money management, major examination assumes a significant part. Financial backers evaluate an organization's inborn worth by looking at variables like income, profits, and development possibilities. The objective is to buy stocks exchanging underneath their characteristic worth.

5.2 Development Contributing

5.2.1 Seeking after Learning experiences

Development contributing spotlights on organizations with solid potential for better than expected profit development. Companies with growing revenues, innovative products, and the capacity to capture market share attract investors' attention. Development financial backers are many times ready to pay a premium for stocks with high development potential.

5.2.2 Assessing Development Stocks

Examining factors like income development rates, profit development, and future possibilities is fundamental in development contributing. Financial backers may likewise consider problematic advances, market patterns, and the serious scene while recognizing potential development stocks.

5.3 Income Investing

5.3.1 Producing Passive Income

The goal of income investing is to produce a steady stream of passive income through dividends and interest. Financial backers frequently target profit paying stocks or fixed-pay protections like bonds. This procedure is famous among those looking for normal pay, like retired people.

5.3.2 Examining Dividend Stocks In order to pursue income investing, it is essential to examine a company's dividend history, payout ratio, and dividend sustainability. Expanding across areas and picking stocks with a background marked by stable profits improves the pay financial backer's gamble the executives procedure.

5.4 Force Money management

5.4.1 Riding Business sector Patterns

Force money management includes gaining by existing business sector patterns. Stocks that have performed well recently are bought by investors who anticipate that the trends will continue. Energy methodologies frequently require continuous observing and speedy navigation.

5.4.2 Specialized Examination in Energy Contributing

Specialized pointers, diagram examples, and cost patterns are integral to energy contributing. Brokers utilizing this system depend on devices like moving midpoints, Relative Strength File (RSI), and trendlines to distinguish section and leave focuses in view of the stock's new cost developments.

5.5 Antagonist Contributing

5.5.1 Conflicting with the Group

Antagonist financial backers intentionally conflict with winning business sector feeling. They anticipate a future reversal and look for opportunities in stocks that are undervalued or have lost popularity. Contrarian investing necessitates perseverance and the conviction that market mispricing will eventually correct.

5.5.2 Gamble the executives in Antagonist Contributing

Antagonist financial backers should cautiously oversee gambles related with conflicting with the market agreement. Laying out clear passage and leave measures, enhancing across different antagonist positions, and staying away from exorbitant focus in a solitary stock or area are key gamble the executives standards.

Financial backers frequently consolidate components of these methodologies in view of their monetary objectives, risk resistance, and economic situations.

Fitting your way to deal with line up with your speculation targets is fundamental for building a balanced and strong portfolio. The ensuing segments will dig into investigating explicit stocks; risk the executives systems, and the devices and stages accessible for fruitful securities exchange money management.

5. Venture Systems

5.1 Worth Money management

5.1.1 Standards of Significant worth Money management

Esteem money management includes distinguishing underestimated stocks and putting resources into them with the assumption that their actual worth will be perceived after some time. Analyzing financial statements, looking for businesses with a margin of safety, and focusing on long-term holding are key principles.

5.1.2 Principal Examination in Worth Financial planning

In esteem effective money management, major examination assumes a significant part. Financial backers evaluate an organization's inborn worth by looking at variables like income, profits, and development possibilities. The objective is to buy stocks exchanging underneath their characteristic worth.

5.2 Development Contributing

5.2.1 Seeking after Learning experiences

Development contributing spotlights on organizations with solid potential for better than expected profit development. Companies with growing revenues, innovative products, and the capacity to capture market share attract investors' attention. Development financial backers are many times ready to pay a premium for stocks with high development potential.

5.2.2 Assessing Development Stocks

Examining factors like income development rates, profit development, and future possibilities is fundamental in development contributing. Financial backers may likewise consider problematic advances, market patterns, and the serious scene while recognizing potential development stocks.

5.3 Income Investing

5.3.1 Producing Passive Income The goal of income investing is to produce a steady stream of passive income through dividends and interest. Financial backers frequently target profit paying stocks or fixed-pay protections like bonds. This procedure is famous among those looking for normal pay, like retired people.

5.3.2 Examining Dividend Stocks

In order to pursue income investing, it is essential to examine a company's dividend history, payout ratio, and dividend sustainability. Expanding across areas and picking stocks with a background marked by stable profits improves the pay financial backer's gamble the executives procedure.

5.4 Force Money management

5.4.1 Riding Business sector Patterns

Force money management includes gaining by existing business sector patterns. Stocks that have performed well recently are bought by investors who anticipate that the trends will continue. Energy methodologies frequently require continuous observing and speedy navigation.

5.4.2 Specialized Examination in Energy Contributing

Specialized pointers, diagram examples, and cost patterns are integral to energy contributing. Brokers utilizing this system depend on devices like moving midpoints, Relative Strength File (RSI), and trendlines to distinguish section and leave focuses in view of the stock's new cost developments.

5.5 Antagonist Contributing

5.5.1 Conflicting with the Group

Antagonist financial backers intentionally conflict with winning business sector feeling. They anticipate a future reversal and look for opportunities in stocks that are undervalued or have lost popularity. Contrarian investing necessitates perseverance and the conviction that market mispricing will eventually correct.

5.5.2 Gamble the executives in Antagonist Contributing

Antagonist financial backers should cautiously oversee gambles related with conflicting with the market agreement. Laying out clear passage and leave measures, enhancing across different antagonist positions, and staying away from exorbitant focus in a solitary stock or area are key gamble the executives standards.

Financial backers frequently consolidate components of these methodologies in view of their monetary objectives, risk resistance, and economic situations. Fitting your way to deal with line up with your speculation targets is fundamental for building a balanced and strong portfolio. The ensuing segments will dig into investigating explicit stocks, risk the executives systems, and the devices and stages accessible for fruitful securities exchange money management.

6. Investigating Stocks

6.1 Association Financials

6.1.1 Compensation Explanation

Taking apart the compensation declaration gives encounters into an association's wages, expenses, and efficiency. Income growth, net and net overall revenues, and profit per share (EPS) are important metrics. Understanding these figures surveys an association's money related prosperity and execution.

6.1.2 Monetary record An organization's resources, liabilities, and value are totally recorded on the asset report. Monetary benefactors assess liquidity extents, similar to the continuous extent, and impact extents to gauge financial strength. Examining an association's commitment levels and asset creation is crucial for getting a handle on its money related development.

6.1.3 Pay Clarification

Pay clarifications uncover how an association makes and uses cash

6.2 Industry Assessment

6.2.1 Market Examples

Understanding industry designs is essential for surveying an association's merciless position. By analyzing market dynamics, growth prospects, and potential disruptors, investors can make more educated decisions regarding a company's future prospects within its sector.

6.2.2 Serious Scene

Investigating an association's adversaries gives setting to its market position. Financial backers have an easier time assessing a stock's overall engaging quality when they are aware of the central players, their strengths and weaknesses, and the potential development of the business scene.

6.3 Administration and Initiative

6.3.1 Chief Initiative It is essential to evaluate the wisdom, history, and vital vision of the supervisory team. A fit and visionary drive bunch will undoubtedly investigate challenges and gain by important entryways, decidedly influencing an association's long conceivable outcomes.

6.3.2 Corporate Organization

Assessing an association's corporate organization practices ensures that the organization works directly and ethically. Looking at board structure, pioneer compensation, and financial backer honors gives encounters into the association's commitment to sound corporate organization.

6.4 Trends in the Market and News Patterns

6.4.1 Staying Informed Monitoring trends in the market and news is essential for staying informed about an organization's external environment. Because stock performance can be impacted by significant developments, industry news, and emerging trends, real-time awareness is essential for effective decision making.

6.4.2 Inspecting Business area Feeling

Market assessment, impacted by news and online diversion, can impact stock expenses. Financial backers are better able to anticipate potential price changes and modify their positions when they have a better understanding of opinion hints and the larger market state of mind.

6.5 Investigation Gadgets and Stages

6.5.1 Web based Agent Stages

Utilizing on the web business stages gives permission to ceaseless stock data, research reports, and examination contraptions. To assist financial backers with pursuing informed choices, various stages give instructive assets, market experiences, and adaptable dashboards.

6.5.2 Stock Screeners

Stock screeners help monetary supporters with isolating stocks considering unequivocal measures, for instance, market cap, P/E extent, or benefit yield. This streamlines the assessment cycle, allowing monetary supporters to recognize potential entryways that line up with their endeavor system.

6.5.3 Scientific Devices To lead top to bottom investigations, modern financial backers regularly utilize insightful apparatuses like monetary displaying programming, graphing applications, and algorithmic exchanging stages. These devices give advanced features to exhaustive stock

assessment and philosophy improvement.

To pursue all around informed speculation choices, it is fundamental for integrate broad investigation into the stock determination process. Financial backers can establish a solid foundation for effective securities exchange and effective financial planning by examining the financials of the company, industry factors, initiative quality, remaining informed about market shifts, and utilizing research tools. The subsequent sections will investigate risk management strategies, common mistakes to avoid, and available instruments and platforms for trading securities.

7. Risk The board
7.1 Expansion
7.1.1 Spreading Ventures

Expansion includes spreading ventures across various resource classes, areas, and geographic districts. By staying away from overconcentration in a solitary stock or area, financial backers can relieve the effect of poor-performing resources on the general portfolio.

7.1.2 Resource Distribution

Vital resource designation, taking into account the extent of interests in stocks, bonds, and money, helps balance chance and return. Designating resources in light of speculation objectives, time skyline, and chance resistance adds to a very much expanded portfolio.

7.2 Stop-Misfortune Orders

7.2.1 Drawing Value Lines

Stop-misfortune orders are pre-characterized directions to sell a stock when it arrives at a particular cost level. This hazard the executives device helps limit expected misfortunes via consequently setting off a deal when the stock's worth drops to the foreordained stop-misfortune cost.

7.2.2 Changing Stop-Misfortune Orders

Financial backers ought to consistently reevaluate and change stop-misfortune orders in light of changes on the lookout, stock execution, and individual gamble resistance. Occasional changes guarantee that stop-misfortune orders stay compelling in safeguarding capital.

7.3 Position Estimating

7.3.1 Computing Position Size

Position estimating includes deciding how much capital distributed to a particular speculation. By controlling the size of each position comparative with the general portfolio, financial backers can oversee risk and stay away from extreme openness to individual stocks.

7.3.2 Carrying out a Gamble Rate

Setting a gamble rate for each exchange or position normalizes position measuring. For instance, restricting each exchange to a 2% or 5% gamble of the all out portfolio esteem guarantees that misfortunes are controlled, safeguarding capital for future venture open doors.

7.4 Supporting Systems

7.4.1 Choices and Subsidiaries

Financial backers can utilize choices and different subsidiaries to fence against likely misfortunes. For instance, buying put choices can give a type of protection against a decrease in the worth of a stock. These methodologies assist with overseeing disadvantage risk while keeping up with openness to possible potential gain.

7.4.2 Cash Supporting

For global speculations, cash vacillations can influence returns. Money supporting includes utilizing monetary instruments to counterbalance the impacts of cash developments, diminishing the gamble related with changes in return rates.

7.5 Ordinary Portfolio Survey

7.5.1 Checking Execution

Consistently inspecting portfolio execution permits financial backers to evaluate the viability of their gamble the board systems. Checking individual stock execution, breaking down resource distribution, and changing positions add to keeping a versatile portfolio.

7.5.2 Rebalancing

Market developments can change the underlying resource designation of a portfolio. Occasional rebalancing includes changing the blend of resources for align it back with the planned allotment. This guarantees that chance levels stay steady with the financial backer's gamble resilience.

One of the most important aspects of successful investing is risk management. By broadening ventures, utilizing stop-misfortune orders, measuring positions suitably, utilizing supporting methodologies, and directing ordinary portfolio surveys, financial backers can explore the intrinsic vulnerabilities of the securities exchange while saving capital and upgrading long haul returns. The accompanying segments will investigate normal mix-ups to keep away from and give extra assets to additional learning and improvement in the domain of financial exchange money management.

8. Instruments and Stages for Hypothesis

8.1 Internet based Sellers

8.1.1 Choosing a Dependable Vendor Choosing a legitimate web-based vendor is essential for doing stock trades. Parts to consider coordinate commission costs, convenience, research instruments, and client organization. Outstanding online experts coordinate E*TRADE, TD Ameritrade, and Charles Schwab.

8.1.2 Sorts of Records Online dealers offer an assortment of record types, including individual investment funds, retirement accounts (IRAs), and instruction investment accounts (ESAs). The kind of record you pick relies upon your monetary objectives and obligations.

8.2 Trading Stages

8.2.1 Simple Signs of Collaboration Trading stages provide financial customers with a means of communication to execute trades, access market data, and conduct specific research. The trading experience is further enhanced by simple stages with customizable dashboards, continuous explanations, and advanced graphing instruments.

8.2.2 Flexible Applications A lot of sellers give convenient applications that let monetary supporters trade while they're in a rush. Monetary supporters can remain related with the market in an accommodating way in light of the steady updates, demand execution limits, and portfolio following introduced by flexible applications.

8.3 Stock Screeners

8.3.1 Changed Searches Stock screeners help monetary benefactors in directing and diminishing stocks as per clear standards. Adaptable pursues can merge factors like market capitalization, P/E degree, benefit yield, and focused pointers.

8.3.2 Head and Focused Measures

Stock screeners manage both essential and specific financial supporters. Critical models could coordinate compensation headway and obligation to-regard degrees, while specific standards could consolidate moving midpoints and relative strength markers.

8.4 Authentic Mechanical congregations

8.4.1 Cash related Showing Programming

Present day money related support as frequently as conceivable utilize monetary showing programming to arrange all over assessments. To help hypothesis decisions, these mechanical assemblies work with complex money related showing, circumstance assessment, and valuation assessments.

8.4.2 Charting Applications

Charting applications give progressed specific assessment limits. Financial allies can utilize highlights, for example, trend lines, markers, and overlays to investigate regard upgrades and pursue informed choices.

8.5 Enlightening Assets

8.5.1 Online classes and Instructive exercises

Different electronic experts offer instructive assets, remembering for the web courses, instructive exercises, and articles. These materials cover subjects like money related exchange nuts and bolts, specific assessment, and hypothesis techniques, giving huge experiences to financial support at all levels.

8.5.2 Goal Social class

The ability to connect with peers, share experiences, and gain knowledge is made possible by joining online adventure groups and conversations. Stages like StockTwits, Reddit's financial orchestrating associations, and concentrated discussions permit potential chances to learning and thought trade.

8.6 Financial News Sources

8.6.1 Continuous Market Updates

reaching reliable financial news sources is essential for staying up to date on market developments. Areas, cash related news channels, and committed monetary news applications offer consistent updates, evaluation, and master examination.

8.6.2 Market Appraisal Reports

Research reports from monetary foundations, trained professionals, and trading associations give all over market evaluation. These reports provide crucial experiences for making informed decisions and cover specific stocks, regions, and market designs.

A major move toward fostering a proficient technique for trade cash the executives is choosing the proper endeavor gadgets and stages. A blend of reliable web-based specialists, dynamic trade stages, logical instruments, and instructive assets can further develop your general undertaking understanding, whether or not you are centered around directing trades, driving exploration, or staying taught. The ensuing segments will inspect normal errors to stay away from and add extra assets to a reasonable comprehension of protections trade compelling cash the executives.

9. Ordinary Stumbles to Avoid

9.1 Significant Monetary preparation

9.1.1 Overcompensating to Market Insecurity

Significant cash the executives, driven by fear or excitement, can provoke careless decisions during market differences. Avoid the mistake of making adventure choices considering transient sentiments instead of a goal, long stretch framework.

9.1.2 Seeking after Execution

Monetary supporters regularly make the bungle of seeking after past execution, buying stocks that have actually overflowed. In any case, true execution isn't by and large trait of future accomplishment. It's basic to lead concentrated investigation and make an effort not to seek after decisions solely established on late examples.

9.2 Shortfall of Development

9.2.1 Concentrated Positions Overconcentration in a lone stock or region opens monetary sponsor to raised risk. In the event that a venture performs ineffectively, neglecting to enough expand can bring about critical misfortunes. Extension helps spread chance and gives a more changed portfolio.

9.2.2 Disregarding Resource Designation Overlooking resource distribution can bring about a portfolio that isn't adjusted. Monetary supporters should regularly assess their asset piece to promise it lines up with their bet versatility, adventure targets, and financial circumstances.

9.3 Dismissing Charges and Expenses

9.3.1 High Trading Costs

Ceaseless trading and high trade costs can break down theory returns. To increase their venture's profits, financial backers should be aware of the costs associated with trading stocks and think about low-cost exchange options.

9.3.2 Resource The board Charges

Monetary sponsor in shared resources or exchange traded saves (ETFs) should realize about organization costs. Significant expense extents can essentially influence returns after some time, by and large. Long-term investment results can be improved by selecting low-cost assets.

9.4 Not Thinking About and Changing

9.4.1 Set-and-Failure Mentality

Adopting a set-and-failure mentality without regularly reevaluating projects can result in missed opportunities or exposure to unjustifiable risks. Reliably study your portfolio, change your asset allocation, and stay informed about changes in monetary circumstances.

9.4.2 Powerlessness to Acquire from Slips up

Messes up are significant for the endeavor. Regardless, failing to acquire from these blunders and repeating them can obstruct long stretch accomplishment. Embrace a steady learning viewpoint, search for input, and refine your hypothesis technique for a really long time.

9.5 Market Timing

9.5.1 Trying to Time the Market

Market timing, expecting the particular section or leave centers, is broadly troublesome. Financial backers regularly wrongly attempt to "purchase low and sell high," however it is hard to accurately reliably time occasions. Taking everything into account, base on a controlled, long stretch theory approach.

9.5.2 Answering Fleeting News

Answering thoughtlessly to flashing news can incite unfortunate decisions. Instead of constantly reacting to ad vacillations, financial backers ought to distinguish between agitation and significant data, taking into account the long-term fundamentals of their projects.

Discipline, a thoroughly examined procedure, and a guarantee to progressing learning are fundamental for keeping away from these normal blunders. By managing sentiments, growing, truth be told, monitoring charges, staying informed, and avoiding market timing traps, monetary supporters can further develop their conceivable outcomes manufacturing an intense and powerful endeavor portfolio. The going with regions will offer additional resources and course for those wanting to refine their monetary trade successful cash the board capacities moreover.

10. Developing a Long-Term Portfolio

10.1 Define Your Investment Goals

10.1.1 Clear Goals The first step is to define clear, attainable investment goals. Whether it's setting something to the side for retirement, sponsoring guidance, or making monetary prosperity, your targets will shape the plan of your portfolio and guide your endeavor decisions.

10.1.2 Time Skyline Consider your time line for each goal. Long-term goals may necessitate a more development-focused approach, whereas short-term objectives may necessitate a more risk-free venture approach. Adapt your portfolio to the time frames of your financial objectives.

10.2 Review Chance Strength

10.2.1 Sorting out Possibility

Evaluate your bet opposition by pondering components like your financial situation, adventure data, and near and dear strength. Your bet strength influences the mix of assets in your portfolio and how you approach flightiness.

10.2.2 Finding a Harmony among Hazard and Return Attempt to track down a harmony among chance and return. Make an effort not to be unnecessarily moderate, which could confine potential returns, and moreover be careful about outlandish bet taking, which can provoke immense hardships. Your portfolio should reflect a pleasant amicability among possibility and potential awards.

10.3 Expanding Strategies

10.3.1 Asset Classes

Grow across asset classes, similar to stocks, securities, and cash reciprocals. Portfolio risk is generally reduced because each resource class responds uniquely to economic conditions.

10.3.2 Geographic and Region Improvement

Geographic and region improvement further mitigates risk. Increased stability and protection against district- or industry-specific slumps can be achieved through an internationally diversified portfolio and an openness to new areas.

10.4 Sensible Monetary preparation

10.4.1 Normal, Social, and Organization (ESG) Measures

Consider coordinating practical monetary arranging guidelines by surveying associations considering normal, social, and organization rules. Adapting your projects to your characteristics can improve their long-term maintainability.

10.4.2 Impact Compelling cash the board

Examine impact successful cash the board open entryways that hope to deliver positive social and biological outcomes nearby financial returns. Impact monetary arranging grants you to add to huge causes while making monetary force.

10.5 Standard Portfolio Review

10.5.1 Discontinuous Assessments

Reliably review your portfolio to promise it lines up with your goals and chance strength. Dissect the presentation of individual property, rebalance as needs be, and change as your monetary conditions or economic situations change.

10.5.2 Expense Viable Methodologies

Consolidate charge compelling techniques to diminish your portfolio's taxation rate. Use charge advantaged accounts and consider charge compelling theory vehicles to smooth out after-evaluation structures.

10.6 Stay Informed and Change

10.6.1 Market Components

Stay informed about money related conditions, market examples, and global new developments. You can change your portfolio system in light of moving conditions by adopting a proactive strategy to showcase elements.

10.6.2 Persistent Learning Invest time and effort into persistent learning to stay current on project systems, market developments, and developing financial scenes. A guarantee to advancing tutoring positions you to make informed decisions in strong business areas.

Building a prudent portfolio requires wary planning, a controlled strategy, and a vow to changing your dares to your characteristics and goals. You can create a portfolio that lasts and adds to your long-term financial success by defining clear goals, assessing risk resiliency, broadening, considering manageable money management, leading regular portfolio surveys, and remaining informed. The subsequent fragments will provide additional resources and guidance to those wanting to broaden how they could decipher doable monetary preparation and portfolio the leaders.

11. Checking and Leaving Positions

11.1 Customary Portfolio Noticing

11.1.1 Following Execution

Reliably screen the show of your portfolio to assess the overall sufficiency of your endeavors. Screen how individual stocks, resources, and asset classes are performing relative with your suspicions and targets.

11.1.2 Rebalancing In order to maintain your ideal resource allocation, periodically rebalance your portfolio. Market improvements can provoke the degrees of different assets in your portfolio to move, and rebalancing ensures that your endeavors line up with your bet versatility and targets.

11.2 Leave Frameworks

11.2.1 Clear Leave Rules

Spread out clear leave measures for each endeavor. Describe the conditions under which you would contemplate selling a stock or leaving a position. This could consolidate hitting a specific expense target, changes in the association's essentials, or a reassessment of your endeavor recommendation.

11.2.2 Bet The chiefs Triggers

Set risk the chiefs triggers to protect your capital. If a stock or adventure shows up at a fated level of mishap, contemplate proposing to confine further mischief to your portfolio. During times when the market is unpredictable, this guarantees that emotions will not influence decisions.

11.3.1 Organization Financials

Watch out for the monetary prosperity of the organizations in your portfolio.

11.3 Major Changes

If there are colossal changes in an association's financials, for instance, declining pay, extending commitment, or debilitating advantage, rethink whether it really lines up with your theory goals.

11.3.2 Organization Changes

Center around changes in boss organization. Reconsidering your investment could be a sign if there are shifts in the supervisory group that raise concerns about the company's direction or important decisions.

11.4.1 Monetary Pointers

Consider more extensive financial pointers and market patterns. Change your portfolio because of indications of a critical monetary slump or primary changes on the lookout. You can make better decisions by keeping an eye on the macroeconomic situation.

11.4.2 Industry Examples

Stay informed about industry examples and unsettling influences. Changes in advancement, customer direct, or authoritative circumstances can influence unequivocal regions. Leaving positions in organizations defying headwinds or changing in accordance with emerging examples is fundamental for a proactive strategy.

11.5.1 Expense Proficiency

While leaving a position, consider charge contemplations. Long stretch capital increments are regularly charged at a lower rate than transient increases. Understanding the cost repercussions of selling an endeavor can help with smoothing out your overall obligation procedure.

11.5.2 Get-together Incidents and Gains

Consider charge setback get-together to adjust gains and breaking point charge commitment. In addition, high duty rates can be exploited by utilizing essential assessment gain reaping. Your generally speaking monetary arrangement ought to be viable with the two systems.

11.6.1 Constant Market Investigation

Constantly analyze economic conditions and news that may have an impact on your businesses. Staying informed grants you to change your portfolio method considering changing circumstances and emerging entryways.

11.6.2 Increase for a reality

Study your past endeavor decisions, both productive and inadequate, to acquire indeed. Your future venture systems can be affected by your cognizance of the elements that added to the two additions and misfortunes.

Noticing and leaving positions require a limited technique, informed route, and a guarantee to changing in accordance with changing financial circumstances. Financial backers can streamline their portfolio for long haul accomplishment by routinely surveying portfolio execution, laying out clear leave standards, taking into account principal changes, staying mindful of economic situations, considering charge contemplations, and gaining as a matter of fact. Those who want to improve their ability to interpret portfolio executives and market elements will benefit from the subsequent segments, which will provide additional assets and direction.

12. Additional Resources

12.1 Books on Stock Market Investing

Benjamin Graham's "The Intelligent Investor": An exemplary aide on esteem effective financial planning and hazard the board.

Burton Malkiel's "A Random Walk Down Wall Street": Investigates different speculation procedures and the productive market speculation.

"Normal Stocks and Exceptional Benefits" by Philip Fisher: Centers around subjective parts of financial planning and company investigation.

"One Up On Money Road" by Peter Lynch: Offers bits of knowledge into

Lynch's venture theory and way to deal with stock picking.

"The Little Book That Actually Beats the Market" by Joel Greenblatt: Presents the idea of the "enchantment equation" for stock financial planning.

12.2 Investopedia's Online Learning Platforms:

Gives extensive instructive substance on different monetary points, including financial planning and exchanging.

Morningstar: Offers venture examination, investigation, and instructive assets for financial backers.

Khan Institute - Money and Capital Business sectors: Gives free seminars on money and capital business sectors, appropriate for fledglings.

Coursera: Offers courses from colleges and foundations overall on money, effective financial planning, and related points.

LinkedIn Learning: Highlights seminars on speculation methodologies, monetary examination, and market patterns.

12.3 Monetary News and Examination Sites

Bloomberg: A worldwide monetary news stage with continuous market information and investigation.

CNBC: Gives business news, monetary data, and market refreshes.

Monetary Times: Offers global business and monetary news, investigation, and reports.

Yippee Money: a platform with stock quotes, charts, and analysis that covers all aspects of financial news and data.

Looking for Alpha: A publicly supported stage for financial exchange examination, news, and conversation.

12.4 Speculation Stages and Instruments

E*TRADE: A web-based financier stage with a scope of venture devices and assets.

TD Ameritrade: provides educational resources and research

tools in addition to a robust trading platform.

Intuitive Merchants: provides access to global markets and a comprehensive set of trading tools.

Fidelity: A full-administration business with an easy to understand stage and examination assets.

Robinhood: A sans commission exchanging stage with a basic and natural point of interaction.

12.5 Monetary Digital recordings

The Diverse Dolt Webcast: Examines securities exchange patterns, venture techniques, and company investigation.

The Podcast for Investors: Investigates different financial planning ideas and highlights interviews with fruitful financial backers.

Planet Cash: A NPR digital recording that makes sense of perplexing monetary and monetary themes in a connecting way.

Bloomberg Experts in Business: Interviews with compelling figures in the money and contributing world.

The Ed Mylett Show: Covers a scope of points, including achievement, initiative, and monetary techniques.

These resources cater to various levels of expertise and cover a wide range of subjects. Whether you're a fledgling hoping to comprehend the essentials or an accomplished financial backer looking for cutting edge methodologies, these books, online stages, monetary news sites, and digital recordings can add as far as anyone is concerned and abilities in securities exchange effective money management.

13. Conclusion

To begin investing in the stock market, one must combine knowledge, strategy, and discipline. All through this extensive aide, we've covered key parts of effective financial planning, from figuring out the securities exchange and putting forth venture objectives to directing financial exchange examination, executing different speculation techniques, and building a maintainable portfolio. We provided insight into monitoring and exiting positions, risk management, and mistakes to avoid.

There is no one-size-fits-all approach to successful investing; it includes fitting your way to deal with line up with your monetary objectives, risk resistance, and economic situations. By consolidating central and specialized examination, differentiating your portfolio, and remaining informed about market patterns, you can go with very much educated choices. Furthermore, consolidating risk the executives systems, staying away from normal traps, and constantly gaining from encounters add to long haul achievement.

Recollect that contributing is an excursion that requires continuous instruction and variation to changing business sector elements. Whether you're a fledgling financial backer or somebody hoping to refine your abilities, the assets gave, including books, web based learning stages, monetary news sites, venture instruments, and digital broadcasts, can act as important aides on your speculation way.

As you explore the intricacies of the financial exchange, stay patient, remain trained, and embrace the valuable open doors for development and learning. Contributing is a dynamic and compensating pursuit that, with cautious preparation and smart execution, can contribute essentially to your monetary prosperity. May your speculation process be productive and loaded up with informed choices that lead to long haul achievement. Cheerful financial planning!